If I Were a Bee

Bethan Jay

For Helena & Robert
in memory of Gabi.

Other books by Bethan Jay:

Gabriel
The Water Wheel Pirates: The tiniest Man
The Waffle Makers
The Alphabet Rhyme

With many thanks to:
Dr. Rolf Gerdes of the 'Starnberg Beekeepers Association'
(and Ilona) for your knowledge and enthusiasm,
Karen McCartney and Matt Smith of 'UK Bees, Wasps and Ants'
and contributors to 'Wir helfen Wildbienen!'
for your amazing bumblebee and solitary bee ID skills,
Fugl Fotos, Book Star, Roc and Heather for all your comments,
Kim Pettit of the 'Spartanburg Beekeepers Association' for
your original photo of a honeybee producing wax,
Alex, Anneke, Christine, Christoph, Claire,
Clare, Dione, Elizabeth, Joni, Maria,
Meike, Petra, Rosie, Sybille and Tanya.

If I were a bee...

I would wake and buzz with glee!

Wiggling

in my hive,

I zummmmm

"hello!"

to you, two, three...

I pop out of the flyhole
then go zooming through the air,

two wings beating each side of me,
a doubly shimmering pair.

I am super cool at flying
but I do not want to brag,

My gangly legs are bendy,
and my knees have 'shopping bags'!

I go whooshing between houses,
over cars...but can you see,

with two hundred beats a second,
that my wings are lifting me?!

Dandelions, bluebells...mmm!
What's blossoming today?

Kilometres, several miles
to buzz ain't far away!

With teeny 'eyes' atop my head
great big ones on both sides,

I spy precious petal patterns
that present my dining guide!

Pollinator Menu:
Follow the lines
to
Geranium Smoothie
or
Passion Flower Drizzle

Red petals don't look red at all,

but other colours 'glow'!

I use my ultra-violet 'specs'
to scan and dart below.

I 'hear' the busy hummmming
of the other bees nearby
as they
flit
between
bright flower heads
and bob in breeze up high.

Vibrations get me going,
buzzes, hums,
in-hive, outside.
My antennae
'smell' and feel things,
bend or pop up as I ride!

I plunge my head into a flower

and suck up with my straw
the sweet, delicious nectar!...

...But I do not leave before
I rub the powdery pollen
on my legs and
round my
knees
and let the plants all pollinate -
while trying not to sneeze!

I whizz back to my beehive fast
to meet with all my mates,

bringing nectar 'goo' and pollen
for the grand communal 'plate'.

We love to work together
and we norm'lly hate to sting.
We'd rather dance and
jiggle round
and share our perfumed 'zing'!

I watch the larvae scoff
'beebread'
of enzymes, pollen, honey,
while nurse-bees squeeze
white jelly out
for younger babes...

...and Mummy!

Or Queenie, as the boss is called.
With her there is no messing -
she's very good at laying eggs

'thousand a day, I'm guessing!

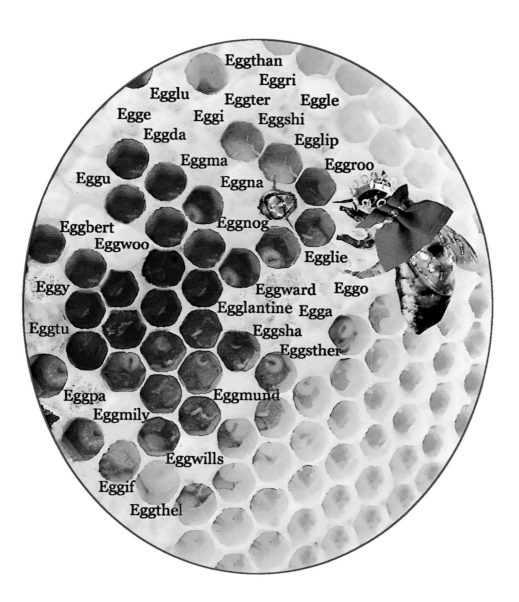

25

I 'try my hand' at chomping
to build more honeycomb
chewing wax scales from my tum
to build our high-rise home.

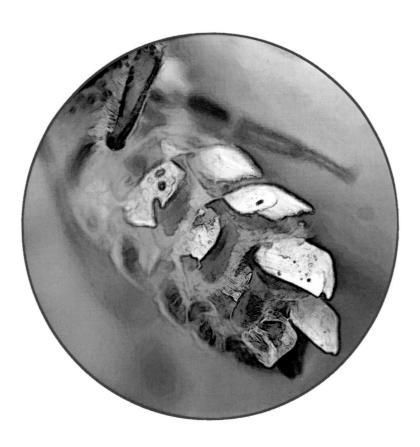

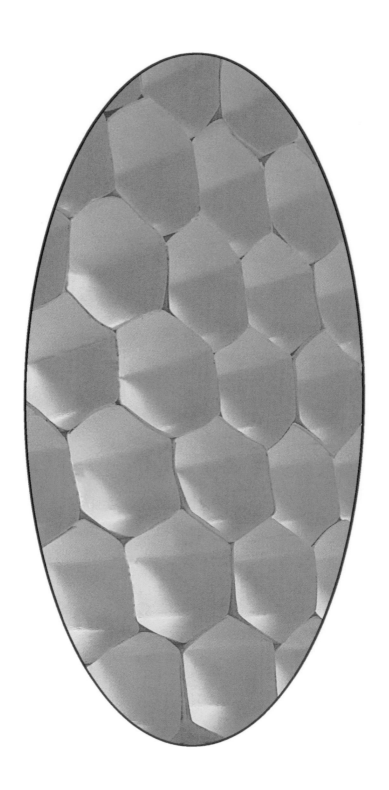

When some little cracks
need fixing,
or the beehive should get chiller,
I make some thick
'propolis-glue'
our wax-sap-spit bee filler.

Next I dob some wax to seal
six-sided tubs of honey -
that's nectar spat and chewed by chums,
wing-fanned 'til it's not runny.

The Original Bee Fan-tastic

I know that 'sicking up' sweet stuff
is not very polite,
but our nectar-honey-tums
produce antibiotic-lite!

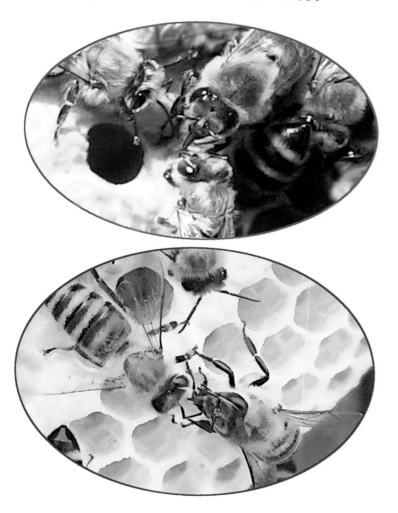

I make so many handy things
to help you through your lives:
candle wax and honey...

bee-pollinated food supplies!

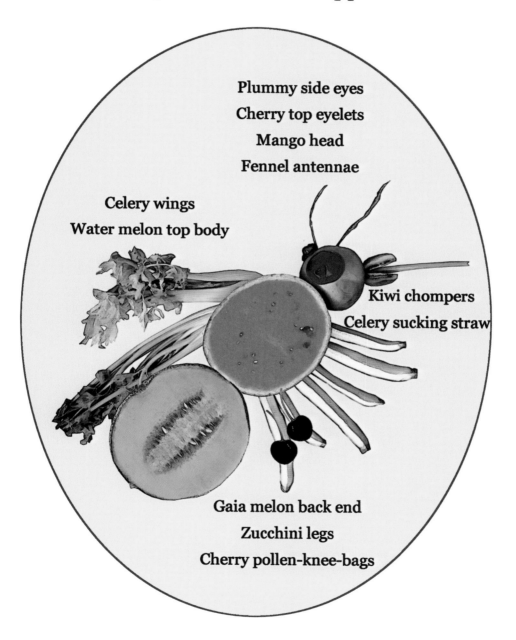

Plummy side eyes
Cherry top eyelets
Mango head
Fennel antennae

Celery wings
Water melon top body

Kiwi chompers
Celery sucking straw

Gaia melon back end
Zucchini legs
Cherry pollen-knee-bags

Now,

for when we're feeling peckish

we've stacked quite a

pile of

treats!

Pollen snacks,

and

honey pie

that's fine and soft and sweet.

So

maybe

you

would also like

to be a bee

one day.

But if you can't...

go spread your toast with

liquid gold

okay!

Wool carder bee

Carpenter bee

Dark earth bumblebee*

Did you know?

We need bees! Without bees it is hard or impossible to pollinate much of our food. And many other creatures rely on bee-pollinated food in the 'food-chain'.

The "If I Were a Bee..." poem is about honeybees. But there are **other bees, called 'bumbles' and 'solitaries'. Solitaries and bumbles are super-pollinators! There are thousands of bee types: tree bumbles, mason bees, carpenter bees, wool carder bees, leaf-cutters...! Have a look over the page.**

Bees help us and we can help them. They need plants for nectar and pollen, water to drink, places to live - including undisturbed areas - and no poisonous pesticides.

If you get a 'bee in your bonnet' about bees, you can plant bee-friendly plants in window boxes or in a garden. You could be a 'busy bee' and, for example, make a 'bee hotel' for some types of solitary bees or a 'bumble bee nest'.

* continental-European version of the British buff-tailed bumblebee

We sometimes say, "a hive of industry".
A beehive can house over 60,000 honeybees in the summer -
with one queen, and thousands of females, known as 'workers'.
A worker has different jobs during its life.
There are also several hundred 'drones' (you can spot one on
page 35). These are male, larger and just eat away -
but die after mating with the queen or
get thrown out of the hive before the winter.

When it rains, bees normally stay at home;
in the winter honeybees snuggle together to keep warm.

Other bees live in medium or small 'colonies', or
in tiny families. They make homes in the ground,
in stems, in trees, in lumps of wood - in all sorts of places.
They need some undisturbed habitat for building nests in.

Many bees press pollen into 'sacks' - hairy curved-in bits
by their knees. There is an expression, "(s)he thinks (s)he's the
bee's knees!" Other bees collect pollen on their tums, legs
or all over their bodies!

Beekeepers harvest some honey from hives,
giving in exchange 'sugar-water' and pressed honeycomb.
People have used honey as food and as a
medicine for thousands of years.
We still also use beeswax, propolis, royal jelly and pollen.

Have you heard of the 'land flowing with
milk and honey', for example in the Bible?
People use the phrase to describe wonderful places!

Orange-tailed mining bee

Leafcutter bee

Mining bee sitting on finger

Yellow-legged mining bee

Orange-tailed mining bee

(Old) common carder bee

Red mason bee

Red mason bee

Masked bee

Ashy mining bee

Mining bee by nest entrance

Hairy-footed flower bee

Hairy-footed flower bee

Bumblebee covered in pollen!

Little flower bee

Little flower bee

Common carder bee

White-tailed bumblebee

Vestal cuckoo bee

Red-tailed bumblebee queen

Tree bumblebee

Buff-tailed bumblebee queen

"After such tastes I'd love to see
the 'land of milk and honey'.
That's where I'd like to end my days -
no rumbling of my tummy!"

"Presenting science in a fun way for children is really important.
Such a good contribution to help raise awareness and
protect our bees."
Friends of the Earth

"Perfect for children and adults who want to know about
life and nature around them. Funny with wordplay & humour."
Amazon Reader Review

"Beautifully worded in rhyme and very educational -
all you and your children should know about bees."
Amazon Reader Review

ABOUT THE AUTHOR
Bethan Jay is a writer and illustrator. She has written for
publishers including Cambridge University Press.
"If I Were A Bee" is her fifth book for children.

Printed in Poland
by Amazon Fulfillment
Poland Sp. z o.o., Wrocław

55443671R00028